# INSPIRING BASKETBALL STORIES FOR KIDS

Fun, Inspirational Facts & Stories For Young Readers

---

## FALCON FOCUS

Copyright © 2023 Falcon Focus

All rights reserved. No part of this publication may be reproduced, distributed or transmitted in any form or by any means, including photocopying, recording, or other electronic or mechanical methods, without the prior written permission of the publisher, except in the case of brief quotations embodied in critical reviews and certain other non-commercial uses permitted by copyright law.

Trademarked names appear throughout this book. Rather than use a trademark symbol with every occurrence of a trademarked name, names are used in an editorial fashion, with no intention of infringement of the respective owner's trademark. The information in this book is distributed on an "as is" basis, without warranty. Although every precaution has been taken in the preparation of this work, neither the author nor the publisher shall have any liability to any person or entity with respect to any loss or damage caused or alleged to be caused directly or indirectly by the information contained in this book.

*Basketball is more than a game; it's a rhythmic symphony echoing on the hardwood floor. Each dribble is a note, every dunk a crescendo, and every three-pointer a stroke of finesse painted through the net. On this court, every assist is a tale of camaraderie, every fast break a showcase of speed, and every play a fusion of strategy and athleticism. In this arena, legends rise, resilience is showcased, and every point scored is a step toward triumph etched in the passion of both players and enthusiasts.*

# Contents

| | |
|---|---:|
| Introduction | v |
| 1. Stephen Curry's Rise to Stardom | 1 |
| 2. Title IX and Women's Basketball | 7 |
| 3. The Magic of Larry Bird and Magic Johnson | 13 |
| 4. Kobe Bryant's Work Ethic | 20 |
| 5. The Heartwarming Story of Jason McElwain | 27 |
| 6. The Dream Team of 1992 | 33 |
| 7. The Inspirational Tale of Coach Jimmy Valvano | 40 |
| 8. LeBron James: From High School Phenom to NBA Superstar | 47 |
| 9. The Story of Yao Ming | 54 |
| 10. The Legend of Michael Jordan | 61 |
| References | 69 |
| Bonus: Free Book! | 71 |

## Introduction

Welcome to the enthralling universe of *Inspiring Basketball Stories For Kids*, a compilation that unravels spellbinding narratives of resilience, courage, and the sheer passion for the game. Within the confines of these pages, you are about to embark on an extraordinary odyssey, delving into the lives of iconic basketball figures and pivotal moments that have etched an enduring imprint on the vibrant canvas of the sport.

Each chapter in this anthology unfolds a distinctive story, casting a spotlight on legendary players and pivotal events that have contributed to the rich tapestry of basketball. From Stephen Curry's dazzling ascent to Larry Bird and Magic Johnson's electrifying rivalry, and the heartwarming story of Jason McElwain to the global impact of Yao Ming, this collection rejoices in the diverse and awe-inspiring facets of basketball.

As we journey through the annals of basketball history, we'll witness Michael Jordan's legendary prowess, the empowering impact of Title IX on women's basketball, and the collective magic of the 1992 Dream Team. Join us in exploring Kobe Bryant's unyielding work ethic, LeBron James' remarkable journey, and the indomitable spirit of Coach Jimmy Valvano, whose inspirational tale transcends the bounds of the court.

Embark on a captivating voyage, from the roots of basketball's evolution to its global expansion and the enduring values of teamwork, dedication, and the relentless pursuit of excellence. These stories extend an invitation to be inspired, to dream, and to embrace the spirit of basketball—one of the world's most thrilling and unifying sports. Let's commence this journey together, where every shot taken and every obstacle overcome paints a vivid portrait of the enduring magic that is basketball.

**Stephen Curry's Rise to Stardom**

## Early Years and College Career

Stephen Curry's journey to becoming an NBA superstar began far from the bright lights of professional basketball courts. Born in Akron, Ohio, on March 14, 1988, and raised in Charlotte, North Carolina, Curry grew up in a basketball family. His father, Dell Curry, was a sharpshooter in the NBA, and this environment nurtured Stephen's love for the game from a young age. Despite his evident talent and basketball lineage, Curry faced challenges early in his career, particularly when it came to gaining the attention of major college basketball programs. His relatively small stature and lean frame raised doubts among college scouts, leading to him being overlooked by top-tier basketball colleges.

Undeterred by this lack of interest from big basketball schools, Curry accepted a scholarship from Davidson College, a small liberal arts school in North Carolina. This decision marked the beginning of an extraordinary college career that would eventually catapult him into the national spotlight. At Davidson, under the guidance of coach Bob McKillop, Curry honed his skills, particularly his now-legendary three-point shooting. He quickly emerged as a force to be reckoned with in the college basketball arena.

In his sophomore year, Curry led the nation in scoring and set a new NCAA record for three-pointers made in a season. His incredible performance caught the attention of basketball fans and analysts across the country. But it was during the 2008 NCAA Tournament that Curry truly announced himself to the world. He led the Wildcats, an underdog team, on a remarkable run to the Elite Eight, showcasing not just his shooting prowess but also his leadership and poise under pressure. This tournament run included a series of high-scoring games against Gonzaga, Georgetown, and Wisconsin, capturing the imagination of basketball fans and elevating Curry to the status of a college basketball sensation.

Curry's time at Davidson was marked not just by his on-court achievements but also by his impact on the college itself. His success brought unprecedented attention and excitement to the school, turning their basketball games into must-watch events and inspiring a wave of 'Curry fever' across the campus. He became a beloved figure at Davidson, admired for his humility and work ethic as much as for his basketball talents. Curry's college career laid the foundation for his future success and set the stage for his transition to the NBA, where he would continue to defy expectations and redefine the game of basketball.

## NBA Draft Skepticism

The 2009 NBA Draft marked a pivotal moment in Stephen Curry's career, yet it was shrouded in uncertainty and skepticism by many basketball analysts and professionals. Despite his remarkable achievements at Davidson, doubts lingered about how his skills would translate to the NBA. The primary concerns centered around his physical attributes. Standing at 6'3" (1.92 meters) and weighing 185 pounds (84 kilograms) at the time, Curry's slender build was considered a significant disadvantage in a league dominated by larger and more physically imposing players. Critics questioned his ability to handle the physicality of the NBA and compete against stronger, faster athletes.

Another major concern was his defensive capability. Scouts and analysts debated whether Curry could hold his own on the defensive end of the court. In college, he was a scoring sensation, but the NBA required a more well-rounded skill set. There were worries that he might become a liability on defense, making it challenging for him to stay on the court in crucial game situations. These doubts were potent enough that several teams with higher draft picks passed on the opportunity to select Curry, uncertain of his potential to succeed at the highest level of basketball.

The Minnesota Timberwolves, in particular, made a notable decision in the 2009 Draft that would later be scrutinized. With the fifth and sixth overall picks, they chose two other point guards, Ricky Rubio and Jonny Flynn, bypassing Curry. This move exemplified the prevailing uncertainty about Curry's ability to excel in the NBA. When the Golden State Warriors selected Curry with the seventh overall pick, it was seen as a gamble, a decision fraught with risk given the prevailing doubts about his physicality and defensive skills.

Curry's selection by the Warriors began a journey filled with challenges and opportunities to prove his critics wrong. As he entered the NBA, the skepticism he faced during the draft would become a driving force in his career, pushing him to work tirelessly on his game, particularly in areas where he was perceived to be weakest. This period of doubt and uncertainty would eventually lead to one of the most remarkable transformations in NBA history, as Curry not only adapted to the league but went on to redefine it with his unique style of play.

## Revolutionizing the Game

Stephen Curry's impact on the NBA can be best described as revolutionary. His extraordinary shooting ability, characterized by a quick release, incredible accuracy, and range that extended well beyond the three-point line, fundamentally changed how the game is played and perceived. Before Curry, three-pointers were often seen as a secondary option in offense. Curry, however, turned the three-point shot into a primary weapon, showcasing its effectiveness and efficiency. His ability to shoot from virtually anywhere on the court stretched defenses in unprecedented ways, forcing teams to rethink their defensive strategies.

Curry's influence extended beyond just his own team, the Golden State Warriors. He inspired a league-wide shift towards a greater emphasis on three-point shooting. Teams across the NBA began to look for players who could shoot from the perimeter, changing the dynamics of player selection and team building. The ripple effect of Curry's style was evident in the increasing number of three-point shots attempted league-wide. His style of play was not just effective; it was also immensely entertaining to watch. Fans were drawn to the excitement of Curry's long-range shots and his ability to make them under pressure.

In the 2015-2016 NBA season, Curry achieved a historic milestone, becoming the league's first-ever unanimous Most Valuable Player (MVP). This accolade was a testament to his incredible performance throughout the season, which included breaking his own record for the most three-pointers made in a single season. He led the Warriors to a record-breaking 73-win season, the most in NBA history. His unanimous MVP selection underscored the unanimous recognition of his extraordinary talents and the impact he had on the game.

Curry's transformation of the NBA was not just about the records he set or the accolades he received. It was about how he inspired a new generation of players and fans. Young players across the globe began emulating his playing style, practicing long-range shooting and ball-handling skills. Curry showed that one didn't need to be the biggest or the strongest athlete on the court to be successful. His success was built on skill, work ethic, and a deep understanding of the game. Through his revolutionary style of play, Curry redefined what was possible in basketball and carved his name as one of the most influential players in the history of the sport.

## Overcoming Injuries

Stephen Curry's path to greatness in the NBA was not without its hurdles, particularly in the form of repeated ankle injuries that posed a significant threat to his career. Early in his tenure with the Golden State Warriors, Curry encountered a series of ankle issues that raised concerns about his durability as a professional athlete. These injuries began to manifest during his second season and became a recurring problem, leading to multiple games missed and surgeries to repair damaged ligaments. The situation was so concerning that it cast a shadow of doubt over his future in the NBA. Critics and fans alike began to question whether his body could withstand the rigors of a full NBA season.

The recurrent ankle problems led Curry and the Warriors' medical staff to explore various rehabilitation and strengthening strategies. This period was marked by intense physical therapy focused on strengthening his ankles and improving his overall physical condition to prevent future injuries. Curry's commitment to his rehabilitation process was a critical factor in his recovery. He dedicated himself to a rigorous and disciplined routine that included targeted exercises to build strength and flexibility in his ankles. This dedication to physical therapy and conditioning was a demonstration of his resilience and determination to overcome the challenges posed by his injuries.

Curry's ability to bounce back from these injuries was not just a physical triumph but also a mental one. He faced the uncertainty and frustration that came with being sidelined and used these challenges as motivation to improve and evolve his game. His experience with injuries taught him the importance of taking care of his body, leading to changes in his training and playing style that would help minimize the risk of future injuries.

The perseverance and dedication Curry showed in overcoming his ankle injuries were integral to his journey toward becoming one of the NBA's elite players. His triumph over these physical challenges served as an inspiring example of resilience and determination. It showed that even the most talented athletes face hurdles, but with the right mindset and work ethic, these obstacles can be overcome. Curry's return to full health and his subsequent achievements in the NBA, including multiple MVP awards and championships, were a direct result of his unwavering commitment to overcoming the injuries that once threatened to derail his career.

# Title IX and Women's Basketball

## Introduction of Title IX

Title IX, a groundbreaking federal civil rights law passed in 1972, marked a significant turning point in the history of women's sports, including basketball. This legislation was signed into law as part of the Education Amendments of 1972 and states, "No person in the United States shall, on the basis of sex, be excluded from participation in, be denied the benefits of, or be subjected to discrimination under any education program or activity receiving Federal financial assistance." The primary aim of Title IX was to end gender discrimination in educational institutions, but its impact went far beyond classrooms and into the realms of athletics.

Before the enactment of Title IX, opportunities for women in sports, particularly at the collegiate level, were limited. Female athletes faced significant disparities in funding, facilities, coaching, and scholarship opportunities compared to their male counterparts. The introduction of Title IX brought a transformative change to this landscape. It mandated equal treatment and opportunities for women in all educational programs and activities, including sports. This law did not specifically mention sports, but its implications for athletic programs were profound.

The passage of Title IX led to a dramatic increase in the participation of women and girls in sports across the United States. Educational institutions, from high schools to colleges, were required to provide equal athletic opportunities to female students. This shift was not immediate and faced resistance in various forms. However, over the years, Title IX has been instrumental in breaking down barriers and leveling the playing field for female athletes.

The impact of Title IX on women's basketball was particularly significant. The law's implementation led to the creation and growth of women's basketball programs across the country. It provided young girls with more opportunities to play the sport from a young age, leading to a rise in the quality and competitiveness of women's basketball at both the high school and college levels. Title IX's influence paved the way for the development of future generations of female basketball players, setting the stage for the successes and popularity that women's basketball enjoys today.

## Impact on Women's Sports

The passage of Title IX in 1972 set off a seismic shift in women's sports, particularly in college athletics, including basketball. Before this legislation, women's sports programs were often underfunded and underappreciated, with limited access to quality coaching, facilities, and equipment. The disparity between men's and women's sports was stark and deeply ingrained in the culture of college athletics. However, Title IX brought about a necessary and overdue change, compelling educational institutions to provide equal opportunities for female athletes.

In the years following the enactment of Title IX, there was a significant and measurable increase in female participation in college sports. The number of women participating in collegiate sports surged dramatically, a direct result of schools striving to comply with the new federal mandate. This surge wasn't just in the number of athletes but also in the diversity of sports available to women. Basketball, in particular, saw a notable rise in popularity and participation. Colleges began investing more in their women's basketball programs, providing better resources, recruiting talented players, and hiring experienced coaches.

The growth in women's college basketball post-Title IX was not just quantitative but also qualitative. The level of competition intensified, and the quality of play improved substantially. Women's college basketball began to attract more attention, not only from sports enthusiasts but also from the general public, which led to increased media coverage and a growing fan base. This heightened visibility helped break down stereotypes and misconceptions about women in sports, showcasing the athleticism, skill, and competitiveness of female basketball players.

Title IX's impact extended beyond the athletes themselves. It created more opportunities for women in coaching, administration, and sports media, contributing to a more inclusive and representative sports culture. The rise in female participation in college sports also had broader societal implications. It empowered young women, giving them confidence and life skills that went beyond the basketball court or athletic field. Participation in sports has been linked to numerous positive outcomes, including higher academic achievement, better health, and increased career success. By opening the doors for more women to participate in college sports, Title IX played a crucial role in advancing gender equality, both in athletics and in broader society.

## Development of the WNBA

The Women's National Basketball Association (WNBA) is a direct and profound legacy of Title IX, representing the pinnacle of professional opportunities in women's basketball. Title IX, by creating an environment where women's sports could thrive at the collegiate level, laid the essential groundwork for the establishment of the WNBA. Before the WNBA's inception in 1997, professional basketball opportunities for women in the United States were limited. The success and growth of women's college basketball, fueled by Title IX, demonstrated the viability and potential of women's professional basketball.

The formation of the WNBA was a landmark moment in the history of sports. It offered female basketball players the opportunity to pursue their dreams at the highest level in their home country, something that was not feasible before. Before the WNBA, many talented female basketball players had to go overseas to find competitive professional play. The establishment of the league was a recognition of the talent, popularity, and commercial potential of women's basketball. It provided a platform for female athletes to showcase their skills on a national stage and to inspire future generations of girls to take up the sport.

The WNBA's inaugural season in 1997 was a significant step forward in women's sports. The league began with eight teams and has since expanded, reflecting the growing interest and investment in women's basketball. The success of the WNBA has been instrumental in elevating the status of the women's game, providing role models for young girls, and proving that women's sports can attract fans and generate revenue. The league has produced some of the most talented and influential basketball players who have become household names, not just within the sports community but across the broader cultural landscape.

The WNBA's impact extends beyond just the professional opportunities it provides for athletes. It has been a platform for social change, with players and the league actively involved in community outreach, advocacy, and initiatives promoting social justice. The WNBA players have been at the forefront of conversations on issues such as gender equality, racial justice, and LGBTQ+ rights, using their platform to raise awareness and drive positive change. The creation of the WNBA, therefore, represents not just the development of a sports league but the emergence of a powerful and influential social institution. It stands as a testament to the progress made since the passing of Title IX and continues to push the boundaries of what is possible for women in sports and society.

## Legacy and Ongoing Challenges

Title IX's influence on women's basketball and sports, in general, has been monumental, but the journey toward gender equality in sports continues to face ongoing challenges. Despite the significant strides made since the enactment of Title IX, disparities still exist in funding, media coverage, and public perception of women's sports compared to men's. Women's sports often receive less investment in terms of facilities, coaching, and promotion, which can affect the development and visibility of female athletes and their sports. These disparities are evident in the differences in salaries, prize money, and sponsorship deals between male and female athletes.

One of the most persistent challenges is the gap in media coverage. Women's sports, including basketball, are significantly underrepresented in sports media. This lack of coverage not only affects the visibility of women's sports but also has a broader impact on public interest and revenue generation. Despite the high caliber of play and the success of leagues like the WNBA, women's basketball still struggles for equal recognition and broadcast time. Increased media coverage is essential for the growth of women's sports, as it helps to build a larger fan base, attract sponsors, and generate more revenue, all of which are essential for the sustainability and development of these sports.

The lasting impact of Title IX on women's basketball is undeniable. It has been a driving force behind the increased opportunities for women in sports, both on and off the field. The rise in the number of female athletes, coaches, and sports administrators is a direct result of this landmark legislation. Title IX has not only opened doors for women in sports but has also contributed to changing societal attitudes toward women and their capabilities. It has shown that given equal opportunities, women can achieve the same levels of excellence and success as men in the athletic arena.

However, the journey towards complete gender equality in sports is an ongoing one. Advocates for women's sports continue to push for better representation, equal pay, and more investment in female athletics. The legacy of Title IX serves as a reminder of the progress made and the work that still needs to be done. It's a call to action for continued advocacy and support for women's sports at all levels. As the landscape of sports continues to evolve, the principles of Title IX remain as relevant as ever, guiding the ongoing efforts to achieve true equality in sports.

# The Magic of Larry Bird and Magic Johnson

## College Rivalry

The rivalry between Larry Bird and Magic Johnson, two of the most iconic figures in basketball history, began not in the NBA, but on the college hardwood in the 1979 NCAA Championship game. This game is often regarded as the genesis of one of the greatest rivalries in sports history and a turning point for college basketball's popularity in the United States. Larry Bird, hailing from the small Indiana State University, had led his team to an undefeated season and into the championship game. On the other side was Earvin "Magic" Johnson, the charismatic leader of the Michigan State Spartans, who had already begun to make a name for himself with his dazzling play and infectious personality.

The 1979 championship game was more than just a clash between two great teams; it was a showcase of two contrasting styles and personalities. Bird, known for his sharpshooting and meticulous playing style, was the quintessential hardworking, blue-collar player. Magic, with his flair for showmanship and exceptional passing ability, brought a level of excitement and dynamism to the game. This game was billed as a showdown between the country's two best college players, drawing unprecedented attention and setting a television ratings record for college basketball that stands to this day.

Indiana State, led by Bird, entered the game with a perfect 33-0 record, while Michigan State, powered by Johnson, had a 25-6 record. The game itself, held at the Special Events Center in Salt Lake City, Utah, drew a packed crowd and millions of viewers on television. Magic Johnson's Spartans emerged victorious, defeating Bird's Sycamores 75-64. Johnson's all-around performance and his team's depth overpowered Bird's individual brilliance. This game was a defining moment in both players' careers, setting the stage for their future battles in the NBA.

The 1979 NCAA Championship game's impact went beyond the final score. It catapulted college basketball into the national spotlight and set the stage for the expansion and popularity of the NCAA tournament, now known as March Madness. The Bird-Johnson rivalry became a captivating narrative that would follow them into their professional careers, adding a new layer of excitement to the NBA. This game is remembered not just for the birth of a rivalry but also for its role in elevating college basketball to a new level of national prominence. Bird and Johnson, through their epic showdown, changed the landscape of basketball, paving the way for the sport's growth in popularity and influence in the years to come.

## NBA Careers and Rivalry

Larry Bird and Magic Johnson's transition to the NBA marked the beginning of a new chapter in their rivalry, one that would define an era in professional basketball. Larry Bird was drafted by the Boston Celtics in 1978, a year before Magic Johnson was picked by the Los Angeles Lakers. Their arrival in the NBA coincided with a period when the league was struggling with low television ratings and waning public interest. Bird and Magic, with their contrasting styles and personalities, quickly became the faces of the NBA, sparking a renewed interest in the league.

Bird's career with the Celtics was characterized by his incredible work ethic, precision shooting, and no-nonsense attitude on the court. He was known for his clutch performances, especially in high-pressure situations, and his ability to elevate the play of his teammates. Bird led the Celtics to three NBA championships (1981, 1984, 1986) and was named the league's Most Valuable Player (MVP) three times consecutively (1984, 1985, 1986). His rivalry with Magic Johnson was most intense during this period, as the Celtics and Lakers frequently faced each other in the NBA Finals.

Magic Johnson's impact with the Lakers was immediate and electrifying. He was known for his extraordinary passing, versatility, and charismatic leadership. Magic led the Lakers to five NBA championships (1980, 1982, 1985, 1987, 1988) and won the MVP award three times (1987, 1989, 1990). His "Showtime" Lakers were known for their fast-paced, entertaining style of play, which contrasted sharply with the more methodical and physical style of Bird's Celtics.

The Celtics-Lakers rivalry, epitomized by Bird and Magic, became one of the greatest in sports history. The teams met in the NBA Finals three times in the 1980s (1984, 1985, 1987), with each encounter adding to the legacy of their rivalry. These matchups were not just battles for NBA supremacy; they were also seen as a clash of East vs. West, blue-collar grit vs. Hollywood glamour, and individual brilliance vs. charismatic leadership. Bird and Magic's rivalry captivated basketball fans around the world and is credited with bringing the NBA into the mainstream of American sports and entertainment.

Off the court, Bird and Magic's relationship evolved from fierce competitors to lifelong friends. Their mutual respect and admiration for each other grew over the years, especially after they retired from professional basketball. They realized that their rivalry had brought out the best in each other and had a profound impact on their personal and professional lives. Bird and Magic's careers and rivalry not only elevated their status as legends of the game but also transformed the NBA, setting the stage for the global popularity it enjoys today. Their story is a testament to the power of sports to unite, inspire, and entertain.

## Impact on the NBA

The rivalry between Larry Bird and Magic Johnson in the 1980s had a profound and lasting impact on the NBA, transforming it into a global phenomenon. At a time when the league was struggling to captivate the wider public, the individual brilliance and contrasting styles of Bird and Magic injected excitement and drama into the game. Larry Bird, with his unmatched shooting ability and meticulous approach, brought a level of skill and precision to the game that was awe-inspiring. His talent for making crucial shots in high-pressure situations made him a fan favorite, especially among supporters who admired the hardworking, disciplined ethos he represented.

Magic Johnson, on the other hand, was a master of the all-around game. His exceptional passing, court vision, and versatility redefined the role of a point guard in basketball. Magic's ability to play multiple positions, including a memorable performance as a center in his rookie season's NBA Finals, showcased his unique skill set. His charismatic personality and the flair with which he played the game made the Lakers' "Showtime" basketball a must-watch spectacle. This entertaining style of play not only drew in die-hard basketball fans but also attracted those who had never before shown an interest in the sport.

The Bird-Magic rivalry became a central storyline of the NBA during the 1980s, capturing the imagination of fans and media alike. Their frequent matchups, especially in the NBA Finals, were highly anticipated events, often billed as the ultimate showdowns in basketball. This rivalry was not just about individual glory; it was a battle for team supremacy that represented two contrasting cultures and philosophies. Bird's Celtics symbolized the traditional, team-oriented approach, while Magic's Lakers were emblematic of a new, fast-paced, and entertaining style of basketball.

The impact of their rivalry on the NBA's popularity was immense. Television ratings for NBA games, particularly during the playoffs and finals, saw significant increases. The league started to attract major sponsorship deals and began its expansion into international markets. Bird and Magic's rivalry laid the foundation for the NBA's transformation into a global entertainment brand. It set the stage for the emergence of future basketball superstars and the expansion of the league's influence beyond the borders of the United States.

In essence, Larry Bird and Magic Johnson did more than just dominate the basketball court; they changed the way the game was perceived and played. Their rivalry brought out the best in each other and in the sport, leading to a golden era in basketball that still resonates with fans around the world. The 1980s are often looked back upon as one of the most exciting and transformative periods in NBA history, a testament to the incredible impact of two of the game's greatest players.

## Friendship and Legacy

The relationship between Larry Bird and Magic Johnson evolved significantly over the years, transitioning from a fierce rivalry on the court to a deep and enduring friendship off it. This transformation began in earnest when they were both selected to represent the United States on the 1992 Olympic Dream Team. The Dream Team, composed of some of the greatest basketball players ever, including Michael Jordan, Charles Barkley, and Karl Malone, is often considered the best sports team ever assembled. Bird and Magic, both near the end of their illustrious careers, were pivotal figures on this team, bringing their experience, leadership, and iconic status to the group.

During the preparations and the Olympics, Bird and Magic's relationship took a new turn. They spent considerable time together, sharing stories, discussing their careers, and reflecting on their long-standing rivalry. This period allowed them to understand and appreciate each other's struggles and triumphs, forging a bond based on mutual respect and admiration. The time they spent as teammates in the Olympics was a healing and unifying experience, transforming their once intense rivalry into a friendship.

Their joint contribution to the Dream Team and the global impact of that team further cemented their legacy in the world of basketball. The Dream Team didn't just dominate the Olympics; it captivated a global audience, spreading the popularity of basketball around the world. Bird and Magic were central to this phenomenon, serving as ambassadors of the sport and showcasing the best of American basketball. Their leadership and charisma were instrumental in the team's success and in promoting the NBA internationally.

After retiring from professional basketball, Bird and Magic continued to share a close bond. Their friendship was tested and strengthened again when Magic announced he was HIV positive in 1991. Bird was one of the first to publicly support him, demonstrating the depth of their relationship. Over the years, they have made joint appearances, often discussing their past rivalry and current friendship, which has become an inspiring story of growth, understanding, and mutual respect.

The legacy of Bird and Magic extends beyond their individual achievements and records. They are credited with revitalizing the NBA during a critical period, inspiring a generation of players and fans, and helping to turn basketball into a global sport. Their transition from rivals to friends is a compelling narrative that adds a human dimension to their legendary status. Their story is not just about basketball; it's about the power of sports to bring people together, to heal divisions, and to forge lasting bonds.

## Kobe Bryant's Work Ethic

## Early NBA Challenges

Kobe Bryant's journey in the NBA, marked by extraordinary success and legendary work ethic, began with a set of challenges that tested his resolve and dedication. Drafted straight out of Lower Merion High School in 1996, Kobe entered the league with high expectations and immense potential. Selected by the Charlotte Hornets with the 13th overall pick and then traded to the Los Angeles Lakers, Kobe's transition to the professional level was not without its difficulties. He was joining a league dominated by seasoned veterans, and as a teenager, he had to adjust not only to the higher level of play but also to the physical and mental demands of the NBA.

In his early years with the Lakers, Kobe faced a unique set of challenges. He was not immediately thrust into a starring role, instead coming off the bench in a team that already had established stars like Shaquille O'Neal. His playing time was limited and his role in the team was not yet defined. Kobe's aggressive playing style and unyielding confidence, while hallmarks of his later success, initially led to criticism. Some viewed him as overconfident and accused him of trying to do too much on the court. His rookie season was marked by a notable low point in the 1997 playoffs against the Utah Jazz, during which he air-balled several crucial shots in a close game. This moment, though a setback, was a turning point for Kobe.

Instead of being deterred by these early challenges and criticisms, Kobe's response was to work harder. He became known for his relentless work ethic, spending countless hours in the gym practicing and refining his skills. His determination to improve was evident in every aspect of his game. He studied film relentlessly, worked on his physical strength, and honed his shooting and ball-handling skills. Kobe's commitment to improvement was not just about outworking his opponents; it was about outworking himself, constantly pushing his limits, and setting new goals.

Kobe's dedication during these early years laid the foundation for his future success. He transformed his weaknesses into strengths and gradually earned a more significant role on the Lakers team. His work ethic became legendary, inspiring not just his teammates but players across the league and generations of future athletes. His journey from a high school prodigy facing early challenges in the NBA to one of the greatest players in the history of basketball is a testament to his unyielding dedication and commitment to excellence. This journey was marked not just by his achievements and accolades but by his relentless pursuit of improvement and his unwavering belief in his ability to overcome any obstacle.

## Relentless Training Regime

Kobe Bryant's legendary work ethic was the cornerstone of his illustrious career. His training regime, marked by intensity, discipline, and an unwavering commitment to excellence, set a new standard in the world of professional sports. Kobe's approach to training was holistic, encompassing not just physical conditioning but also an in-depth study of the game and a relentless pursuit of skill development. He was known for his incredible stamina and ability to train for hours on end without losing focus or intensity.

One of the most notable aspects of Kobe's training was his early morning workouts. He often started his day before dawn, dedicating the quiet hours of the morning to honing his skills. This routine included shooting practice, where he would not leave the gym until he made a target number of shots, pushing himself to perfection. His practice sessions were not just about quantity; they were meticulously planned and executed with a focus on improving specific aspects of his game. Kobe's attention to detail during these sessions was extraordinary, with every drill and exercise designed to simulate game situations.

Kobe's physical conditioning was another key component of his training regime. He worked tirelessly to maintain peak physical fitness, understanding that his body was his most valuable asset as an athlete. His workouts included a mix of strength training, agility drills, and endurance exercises, tailored to ensure that he could withstand the rigors of a long NBA season. Kobe's commitment to his physical health extended to his diet and recovery practices. He was mindful of what he ate and how he took care of his body after games and training sessions, ensuring he was always in the best possible shape to perform.

Beyond the physical aspects of his training, Kobe was also a student of the game. He spent countless hours studying film, analyzing not only his performance but also the tendencies and strategies of his opponents. He had a deep understanding of basketball's nuances, which he used to gain a competitive edge on the court. Kobe's intellectual approach to the game, combined with his physical preparations, made him a formidable player and a strategic thinker on the floor.

Kobe's relentless training regime was a testament to his belief that greatness was earned, not given. He once said, "I can't relate to lazy people. We don't speak the same language. I don't understand you. I don't want to understand you." This mindset was evident in every aspect of his training and preparation. His legendary work ethic not only propelled him to the heights of NBA success but also inspired athletes around the world to pursue their dreams with the same fervor and dedication. Kobe's legacy, therefore, is not just defined by his achievements and accolades but also by the example he set in how to prepare, how to work, and how to relentlessly pursue greatness.

## Overcoming Adversity

Kobe Bryant's career, while marked by extraordinary achievements, was not without its share of setbacks and challenges. His journey was evidence of his ability to overcome adversity, be it in the form of injuries or changes within his team. Kobe's determination and resilience in the face of these obstacles were as integral to his legacy as his scoring titles and championship rings. One of the most significant challenges Kobe faced was injuries. Throughout his 20-year career, he suffered a variety of injuries, but two instances stand out for their severity and their timing.

The first major setback came in the form of a severe Achilles tendon injury in April 2013. This type of injury is often devastating for athletes, and for many, it could have signaled the end of a career, especially for a player in his late 30s like Kobe.

However, his response to this challenge was characteristic of his approach to the game and life. He displayed remarkable resilience, undergoing a rigorous and demanding rehabilitation process. Kobe's dedication to his recovery was a clear reflection of his determination to return to the court, despite the odds being stacked against him.

Kobe's adversity wasn't limited to physical challenges; he also navigated significant changes within the Los Angeles Lakers organization. Throughout his career, the Lakers underwent various transformations, including changes in coaching staff and team rosters. Kobe played with a wide range of teammates and under several different coaches, each bringing new dynamics and challenges. Through all these changes, Kobe remained a constant figure for the team, adapting his game and leadership style as necessary. His ability to perform at a high level, regardless of the circumstances, highlighted his mental toughness and adaptability.

Another instance of Kobe overcoming adversity was his response to the Lakers' struggles in the latter part of his career. As the team went through a rebuilding phase, Kobe's role evolved. He became a mentor to younger players, sharing his knowledge and experience, and helping to shape the next generation of Lakers. Even as his physical abilities were affected by age and injuries, Kobe's impact on the team remained significant. He embraced this new role with the same intensity and passion he had shown throughout his career.

Kobe Bryant's ability to overcome adversity, both on and off the court, added a depth to his legacy that transcends statistics and championships. His career is a narrative of resilience, a story of an athlete who refused to be defined by setbacks, and who instead used them as opportunities to grow and evolve. Kobe's relentless spirit in the face of adversity is a powerful part of his enduring legacy, inspiring not just athletes but people from all walks of life to face their challenges with courage and determination.

## Inspiring a Generation

Kobe Bryant's influence extended far beyond the basketball court; his dedication to the sport inspired a generation of athletes and fans worldwide. Known for his relentless work ethic, competitive spirit, and pursuit of excellence, Kobe became more than just a basketball player; he was an icon that symbolized the pinnacle of athletic aspiration. His "Mamba Mentality," a term he coined to describe his approach to basketball and life, resonated with athletes across various sports, encapsulating a mindset of relentless dedication, resilience, and a never-give-up attitude.

Kobe's impact on young athletes was profound. He was a role model to many, not just for his achievements but for the way he achieved them. His commitment to improvement, attention to detail, and willingness to put in the hard work necessary to succeed inspired countless young players to emulate his approach. From practicing late-night shooting to studying game films, Kobe's methods became a blueprint for those looking to excel in their sports. His influence was evident in gyms, courts, and fields all around the world, where young athletes practiced with a dream of achieving greatness like Kobe.

Beyond aspiring athletes, Kobe's dedication to basketball also captivated fans globally. He brought excitement and flair to the game, creating memorable moments and legendary performances that enthralled audiences. Kobe's ability to perform under pressure, his game-winning shots, and his fearless approach to competition left a lasting impression on fans. His international appeal was significant, helping to grow the NBA's global footprint. Kobe was especially beloved in countries like

China and Italy, where he had personal connections and where he actively engaged with his fan base.

Kobe's influence also extended to how athletes approach the mental and emotional aspects of sports. He openly discussed the importance of mental toughness, focus, and the psychological challenges of competing at the highest level. By sharing his experiences and insights, Kobe helped destigmatize discussions around mental health in sports, encouraging athletes to take a holistic approach to their development.

In retirement, Kobe continued to inspire through his coaching, storytelling, and philanthropic efforts. He dedicated himself to mentoring young players, both in the NBA and in youth sports, sharing his knowledge and passion for the game. Kobe's foray into filmmaking and content creation, including winning an Academy Award for his short film "Dear Basketball," showed his creative side and his desire to inspire through storytelling. His philanthropic work, particularly in supporting youth sports and education, further demonstrated his commitment to empowering the next generation.

Kobe Bryant's legacy as an inspiration to a generation is cemented not only in his achievements as a basketball player but also in the way he lived his life and inspired others to pursue their dreams with passion and dedication. His untimely passing in 2020 was a profound loss, but the impact of his life and career continues to resonate with people around the world, ensuring that his legacy will endure for generations to come.

# The Heartwarming Story of Jason McElwain

## Background and Love for Basketball

The story of Jason McElwain, affectionately known as J-Mac, is one of inspiration, determination, and the unifying power of sports. Jason, a high school student with autism, captured the hearts of millions with his extraordinary moment in a high school basketball game. His journey began in Greece Athena High School in Rochester, New York, where he developed a deep love for basketball. Although Jason's autism presented challenges, it did not diminish his passion for the sport. He found a place in the basketball team, not as a player, but as a devoted and enthusiastic team manager.

As a team manager, Jason's responsibilities included attending practices, helping with equipment, and providing moral support to the team. He was an integral part of the team, known for his unwavering enthusiasm and love for the game. Jason's commitment to the team was evident in every task he undertook, and he quickly became a beloved figure among the players and coaches. His knowledge of basketball was extensive and he often shared insights and strategies with the team, showcasing his understanding of the game.

Jason's passion for basketball went beyond just managing his high school team. He spent countless hours practicing shooting hoops, dreaming of one day playing in a real game. Despite the challenges posed by his autism, Jason never let go of this dream. His dedication to basketball was a source of joy and a way for him to connect with others. For Jason, basketball was more than just a sport; it was a vital part of his life, a platform where he could express himself and be part of a community.

The story of Jason McElwain is a powerful reminder of the impact sports can have on individuals, especially those with disabilities. It highlights how sports can provide a sense of belonging, boost self-esteem, and offer opportunities for personal growth. Jason's role as a team manager and his love for basketball exemplify the inclusive nature of sports and its ability to transcend boundaries. His story is not just about basketball; it's about the power of passion, the importance of inclusion, and the extraordinary potential that lies within every individual.

## The Big Game

The highlight of Jason McElwain's high school basketball journey, which turned him into a national sensation, occurred during an emotional game that transcended the typical high school sports experience. It was February 15, 2006, during a game between Greece Athena High School and Spencerport High School. Jason, usually the team manager, was suited up in a uniform for the first time, as the coach had decided to reward him for his dedication to the team. The crowd was aware of

Jason's love for the game and his dream to play, and there was a palpable sense of anticipation in the air.

As the game progressed, Greece Athena secured a comfortable lead. With about four minutes remaining, the crowd began chanting Jason's name, urging the coach to let him play. Responding to the crowd's enthusiasm, the coach called Jason off the bench. What happened next was nothing short of miraculous. Jason, who had never played in an official game before, missed his first two shots. However, undeterred, he quickly found his rhythm. He went on to score an incredible 20 points in just under four minutes, including six three-pointers. Each shot he made sent the crowd into a frenzy, with teammates and spectators alike cheering wildly.

Jason's final three-pointer, scored just as the game ended, was the climax of this extraordinary moment. The gymnasium erupted in cheers, and Jason was swarmed by his teammates and fans in a spontaneous celebration. The emotion in the gym was overwhelming, as players, coaches, and spectators were moved by the remarkable achievement of this young man who had defied expectations and showcased his talent in the most dramatic fashion.

This game was about more than just a victory in a high school basketball match; it was a moment of triumph over adversity, a demonstration of the power of perseverance, and a celebration of inclusion and determination. Jason McElwain's performance that night became an instant classic in the annals of sports history, a story that went beyond Greece Athena High School and captured the hearts of people nationwide. It was a shining example of what can happen when someone is given a chance to realize their dreams, and it underscored the significant impact sports can have in bringing people together and creating unforgettable moments. Jason's achievement in 'The Big Game' was a powerful illustration of the human spirit's capacity to inspire and uplift, resonating with people from all walks of life.

## National Recognition

The aftermath of Jason McElwain's remarkable performance in the high school basketball game was a whirlwind of national attention and acclaim, a stark contrast to his usual role as the team manager. His story, highlighted by his incredible scoring feat, quickly captured the hearts and imaginations of people across the country. News of his achievement spread rapidly, transcending the world of high school sports and entering the national consciousness. Major news outlets picked up the story, eager to share the tale of the high school student with autism who defied expectations and achieved his dream in such spectacular fashion.

Jason's story was featured on various national television networks, including ESPN, CBS, and NBC. He was invited to appear on numerous talk shows, where he shared his experiences and the emotions of that unforgettable game. These appearances gave Jason a platform to speak about autism and raise awareness about the capabilities and potential of individuals with autism. The media attention also highlighted the positive impact of inclusive practices in schools and sports programs, showcasing how providing opportunities for all students, regardless of their challenges, can lead to extraordinary outcomes.

The accolades for Jason's achievement were numerous. He received awards and recognition from sports organizations and community groups, and even received a phone call from President George W. Bush, congratulating him on his inspiring performance. Jason was also honored at various sports events, receiving invitations to attend games and meet with professional athletes who were moved by his story.

One of the most significant recognitions came from the ESPY Awards, where Jason won the ESPY Award for the Best Moment in Sports. This honor was a testament to the impact of his performance, not just as a sports achievement but as a moment that resonated with people far beyond the realm of basketball. The award ceremony was another opportunity for Jason to share his story and continue to inspire others with his message of hope, determination, and the power of dreams.

The national recognition that Jason McElwain received was about more than just celebrating a high-scoring game. It was about acknowledging the power of inclusion, the importance of community support, and the boundless potential within each individual. Jason's journey from a team manager to a national inspiration is a powerful narrative that continues to motivate and encourage people from all walks of life. His story remains a shining example of how determination, opportunity, and support can combine to create moments of triumph that transcend sports and touch the lives of many.

## Legacy and Impact

The story of Jason McElwain, or J-Mac, transcended the realm of sports, leaving an enduring legacy in its wake, particularly in the context of raising awareness for autism and inspiring individuals with disabilities. His remarkable achievement on the basketball court became a beacon of hope and a source of inspiration for many, especially for families and individuals affected by autism. Jason's story challenged prevailing perceptions about the capabilities of people with autism, showcasing that given the right opportunities and support, they can achieve incredible feats.

J-Mac's sudden rise to fame brought much-needed attention to autism, a condition that affects communication and behavior. His story helped to humanize the condition, moving beyond statistics and medical definitions to showcase the potential and personality of someone living with autism. It sparked conversations about autism in homes, schools, and communities, leading to greater awareness and understanding. His achievement served as a powerful example of what can be accomplished when individuals with disabilities are included and supported in their endeavors.

Moreover, Jason's story has been a source of motivation for people with various disabilities. It underscored the importance of not underestimating the abilities of individuals based on their disabilities. Jason became a symbol of determination and resilience, qualities that resonate with many who face their challenges. His story is a reminder that success and achievement take many forms and that everyone has unique talents and capacities.

The impact of Jason's story was also felt in the realm of education and sports programs, where it contributed to a growing emphasis on inclusive practices. It highlighted the importance of providing equal opportunities for all students, regardless of their physical or neurological conditions. Schools and sports programs were encouraged to rethink their approaches to inclusion, creating environments where all students can participate and excel.

J-Mac's legacy is also evident in the way his story continues to inspire. His narrative has been shared in various forms, including documentaries, news articles, and motivational talks, spreading the message of hope and the power of inclusion. The enduring impact of his story lies in its ability to touch hearts and change minds, fostering a more inclusive and understanding society. Jason McElwain's story is a testament to the extraordinary things that can happen when individuals are given a chance to shine, reminding us of the unlimited potential that lies within each person.

## The Dream Team of 1992

## Formation and Significance

The 1992 US Men's Olympic Basketball Team, famously known as the "Dream Team," marked a historic turning point in the world of international basketball. For the first time, professional players from the National Basketball Association (NBA) were permitted to participate in the Olympics, a decision that forever changed the landscape of the sport. This shift was a result of the International Basketball Federation's (FIBA) decision in 1989 to allow professional players in the Olympics, breaking away from the tradition of featuring only amateur athletes in the Games.

The formation of the Dream Team was a response to the growing global appeal of basketball and the desire to showcase the best talent the sport had to offer on the world's biggest stage. Before 1992, the United States had predominantly sent college players to represent the country in Olympic basketball. However, the disappointing bronze medal finish at the 1988 Seoul Olympics signaled the need for change. The inclusion of NBA players was seen as a way to reclaim dominance in the sport and to demonstrate the unparalleled skill and talent present in American basketball.

The announcement of the Dream Team elicited excitement and anticipation not just in the United States, but around the world. The team was a collection of some of the greatest basketball players ever, including Michael Jordan, Magic Johnson, Larry Bird, and Charles Barkley, among others. The assembly of such a star-studded roster was unprecedented in the history of sports. Each member of the team was not only an exceptional player but also a prominent figure in popular culture, contributing to the team's immense appeal and the media frenzy surrounding it.

The significance of the Dream Team's formation extended beyond the realm of sports. It was a cultural phenomenon that showcased the growing influence of basketball as a global sport. The team was a symbol of American excellence in basketball, and their participation in the Barcelona Olympics was seen as a defining moment in the history of the sport. The Dream Team's presence at the Olympics was about more than just winning gold; it was about showcasing the artistry, athleticism, and competitive spirit of basketball at its highest level. Their participation in the 1992 Olympics marked the beginning of a new era in basketball, one where the sport's best players from around the world could come together and compete on the ultimate international stage.

## Star-Studded Roster

The Dream Team's roster for the 1992 Olympics in Barcelona read like a who's who of basketball legends, a gathering of some of the most talented and celebrated players in NBA history. Headlining this illustrious group was Michael Jordan, widely regarded as the greatest basketball player of all time. Jordan, at the peak of his powers with the Chicago Bulls, brought his relentless competitiveness, scoring prowess, and global star power to the team. His presence on the Dream Team was a significant draw for fans and a daunting prospect for opponents.

Joining Jordan were Magic Johnson and Larry Bird, two players who had defined the NBA in the 1980s with their rivalry and exceptional play. Magic Johnson, from the Los Angeles Lakers, was known for his incredible passing, versatility, and charismatic leadership on the court. Despite having retired from the NBA a year earlier due to his HIV diagnosis, Magic's inclusion in the Dream Team was a testament to his enduring skill and popularity. Larry Bird, the sharpshooting forward from the Boston Celtics, brought his precision, basketball IQ, and a wealth of experience to the team. Bird's participation was especially poignant given his ongoing struggle with back injuries, making his presence in the Dream Team a fitting capstone to his illustrious career.

The roster also included other NBA greats, each a superstar in their own right. Charles Barkley, the charismatic and outspoken forward, brought scoring and rebounding strength, along with his larger-than-life personality. Patrick Ewing and David Robinson provided a formidable presence in the paint, both being exceptional centers known for their defensive prowess and scoring ability. Scottie Pippen, Jordan's teammate at the Bulls, was renowned for his defensive skills and all-around game, while John Stockton and Karl Malone, the dynamic duo from the Utah Jazz, brought their famed pick-and-roll game to the international stage.

Clyde Drexler and Chris Mullin, two of the best wing players of their time, added depth and scoring ability to the team. Rounding out the roster was Christian Laettner, the lone college player selected to join this ensemble of NBA stars. Laettner, who had just led Duke University to back-to-back NCAA championships, was included as a nod to the Olympic tradition of featuring amateur athletes.

The Dream Team's roster was not just a collection of talent; it was a harmonious blend of different playing styles, personalities, and generations. Each player brought something unique to the team, whether it was scoring, defense, leadership, or charisma. The assembly of such an array of talent in one team was unprecedented and has since become the stuff of basketball legend. The Dream Team's star-studded roster was a key factor in the team's success and in the lasting impact they had on the sport of basketball globally. Their legacy extends beyond their Olympic gold medal; they set a new standard for excellence in the sport and inspired a new generation of players and fans around the world.

## Dominance in Barcelona

The Dream Team's performance at the 1992 Barcelona Olympics was a display of overwhelming dominance, the likes of which had never been seen before in international basketball. From the outset, it was clear that this team was in a league of its own, bringing an unprecedented level of skill, athleticism, and star power to the Olympic stage. The team's success was not just in winning the gold medal, but in the manner they achieved it – through a series of performances that showcased their superiority over their opponents.

In every game, the Dream Team exhibited a brand of basketball that was both mesmerizing and ruthless. Their games were less about competition and more about exhibition, as they effortlessly outplayed every team they faced. The gap in skill and execution between the Dream Team and their opponents was starkly evident. They won their games by an average margin of 43.8 points, a statistic that exemplifies their dominance. Their closest game, a 32-point victory over Croatia in the gold medal match, was still a display of their overwhelming superiority.

The Dream Team's style of play was a blend of individual brilliance and cohesive team dynamics. They played with a sense of joy and freedom, often turning games into highlight reels of dunks, no-look passes, and long-range shots. The team was unselfish, with each member willing to pass the ball and share the spotlight. Their games were not just about winning; they were about entertaining the audience and showcasing the beauty of basketball. The Dream Team's approach to the game captivated fans and brought new levels of excitement to the sport.

The impact of the Dream Team's performance at the Barcelona Olympics went beyond the medals they won. They were ambassadors of basketball, showcasing the sport at its highest level and inspiring a global audience. The team attracted massive crowds and media attention, bringing unprecedented exposure to basketball. They were not just athletes competing in an event; they were global superstars elevating the status of basketball on the world stage.

The Dream Team's dominance in Barcelona is remembered as one of the greatest achievements in sports history. Their gold medal victory was a foregone conclusion, but the way they achieved it, with grace, power, and a touch of flair, left a lasting impression. They set a new standard for excellence in basketball and inspired countries around the world to invest in and improve their basketball programs. The legacy of the Dream Team's performance in the 1992 Olympics is still felt today, as it was a pivotal moment in the evolution of basketball into a truly global sport.

## Legacy and Influence

The 1992 Dream Team's impact on international basketball and its global popularity is profound and enduring. Their unprecedented performance in the Barcelona Olympics not only solidified their status as one of the greatest teams ever assembled in sports but also served as a catalyst for the global growth of basketball. The Dream Team's influence extended far beyond the gold medals they won; they left a legacy that reshaped the sport on a worldwide scale.

One of the most significant impacts of the Dream Team was the way they captured the imagination of fans around the world. Their games were not just sporting events; they were spectacles that showcased basketball at its most exciting and skillful. The team's style of play, combined with their charisma and star power, attracted new fans to the sport, many of whom had never followed basketball before. The Dream Team brought a level of excitement and flair to basketball that transcended cultural and language barriers, making the sport more accessible and appealing to a global audience.

The influence of the Dream Team also led to a surge in the popularity of the NBA globally. The presence of NBA stars on the Olympic stage showcased the league's talent and helped to promote the NBA brand internationally. Following the Olympics, there was a significant increase in international broadcasting of NBA games, merchandise sales, and a growing international fanbase. The NBA capitalized on this momentum to expand its global reach, fostering partnerships and launching initiatives to grow the sport in various countries around the world.

Furthermore, the Dream Team's dominance in Barcelona inspired a new generation of international players. Young athletes around the world watched the Dream Team and were inspired to take up basketball. The team's influence contributed to a significant improvement in the quality of international basketball, as players and coaches adopted some of the techniques and strategies showcased by the Dream Team. This led to a more competitive international basketball scene and an increase in the number of international players in the NBA.

The Dream Team's legacy is also evident in the way international basketball tournaments are perceived and valued. Their participation in the Olympics elevated the status of basketball in the Games, making it one of the most anticipated and watched events. The excitement and attention generated by the Dream Team helped to solidify basketball's position as a key sport in the Olympics and other international competitions.

In summary, the Dream Team's lasting impact on international basketball is multi-faceted. They popularized the sport globally, contributed to the NBA's international expansion, inspired a new generation of players, and elevated the status of basketball in the global sports arena. The legacy of the Dream Team extends beyond their victories and medals; they changed the way the world views and plays basketball, making an indelible mark on the sport that continues to be felt to this day.

# The Inspirational Tale of Coach Jimmy Valvano

## Coaching Career and 1983 NCAA Victory

Jimmy Valvano, affectionately known as "Jimmy V," etched his name into basketball history through a blend of charismatic leadership, inspirational coaching, and a remarkable underdog victory in the 1983 NCAA Tournament. Valvano's coaching career was characterized by his energetic and passionate approach to the game, his ability to motivate players, and his undeniable love for basketball. His journey as a coach was marked by several successes, but it was his tenure at North Carolina State University (NC State) that defined his legacy.

Valvano began coaching at NC State in 1980, and by the 1982-83 season, he had built a team that demonstrated both skill and resilience. However, the Wolfpack was not initially favored to win the national championship, making their eventual victory all the more extraordinary. The 1983 NCAA Tournament, often referred to as "March Madness," was where Valvano's coaching prowess truly shone. NC State, as a sixth seed, faced a challenging path through the tournament, but under Valvano's leadership, they defied the odds time and again.

The 1983 championship game against the top-seeded University of Houston, a team known as "Phi Slama Jama" for their high-flying athleticism and dunks, was a David versus Goliath matchup. Valvano's Wolfpack, however, was undaunted. Through a combination of strategic game-planning, relentless defense, and the fostering of a strong belief in his players, Valvano led his team to one of the most memorable upsets in college basketball history. The game's final moments, which culminated in a last-second dunk following a missed shot, have become iconic in the annals of sports, a symbol of achieving the improbable.

The victory in the 1983 NCAA Championship was more than just a triumph in a basketball tournament; it was a testament to Valvano's coaching philosophy. He emphasized the importance of believing in oneself, seizing opportunities, and never giving up, regardless of the circumstances. His coaching style was not just about tactics and techniques; it was about instilling confidence, fostering teamwork, and nurturing a winning mentality. Valvano's ability to connect with his players, to inspire them to perform beyond their perceived limits, was central to the Wolfpack's success.

Jimmy Valvano's 1983 NCAA Championship victory with NC State is a story of perseverance, determination, and the power of belief. It remains an enduring example of what can be achieved with passion, hard work, and an unwavering commitment to one's goals. Valvano's journey and success as a coach continue to inspire coaches and athletes across various sports, embodying the essence of what it means to pursue and achieve a dream against all odds.

## Famous ESPY Speech

Jimmy Valvano's "Never Give Up" speech at the 1993 ESPY Awards is remembered as one of the most stirring and inspirational moments in sports history. Delivered amidst his battle with terminal cancer, Valvano's words transcended the realm of sports and touched the hearts of millions around the world. The speech, marked by its emotional depth, humor, and poignant messages, remains a powerful testament to Valvano's spirit and resilience in the face of adversity.

Standing on the stage at the ESPY Awards, weakened by his illness but undeterred in spirit, Valvano captivated the audience with his charisma and authenticity. He spoke candidly about his battle with cancer, not shying away from the reality of his situation, yet his message was one of hope and the enduring power of dreams. He encouraged everyone to laugh, think, and cry each day, a sentiment that emphasized the fullness of life and the importance of experiencing a range of emotions.

Valvano's speech is perhaps best remembered for its powerful concluding statement, "Don't give up, don't ever give up." These words have become a rallying cry for people facing their challenges, a reminder of the strength and determination inherent in the human spirit. Valvano's insistence on the importance of perseverance, even in the darkest of times, struck a chord with people from all walks of life. He emphasized the importance of having dreams to chase, the necessity of enthusiasm and dedication in pursuing those dreams, and the unwavering belief in the possibility of achieving them.

Beyond its immediate emotional impact, Valvano's speech at the ESPY Awards had a lasting and tangible legacy. During the speech, he announced the creation of The V Foundation for Cancer Research, an organization dedicated to finding a cure for cancer. His call to action, coupled with his personal story, galvanized support for the foundation, which has since raised millions of dollars for cancer research. Valvano's speech transformed his personal struggle into a broader movement for hope and change, inspiring countless individuals to contribute to the fight against cancer.

Jimmy Valvano's ESPY speech is a poignant reminder of the power of words and the impact one individual can have. His message of hope, resilience, and the enduring power of the human spirit continues to resonate and inspire. Valvano's legacy, bolstered by this unforgettable speech, lives on through the work of The V Foundation and the countless lives it has touched. His words at the ESPY Awards are a timeless affirmation of the strength of will and the importance of maintaining hope, even in the face of the most daunting challenges.

## Legacy in Cancer Research

The establishment of The V Foundation for Cancer Research is a pivotal part of Jimmy Valvano's enduring legacy, representing his commitment to the fight against cancer. Founded in 1993, following Valvano's passionate speech at the ESPY Awards, The V Foundation was created with a clear mission: to fund cutting-edge cancer research and to work towards a world where cancer can be defeated. Valvano's battle with cancer and his determination to make a difference in the lives of others suffering from the disease were the driving forces behind the foundation's inception.

The V Foundation, since its establishment, has played a significant role in advancing cancer research. It has become one of the premier organizations in funding cancer research grants nationwide. The foundation operates on the principle that all donated funds go directly to cancer research and related programs, maximizing the impact of every contribution. This approach has enabled The V Foundation to fund a wide range of projects and initiatives, from basic laboratory research to clinical trials and patient care programs.

One of the key aspects of The V Foundation's work is its emphasis on funding young researchers and breakthrough research. The foundation recognizes the importance of supporting the next generation of cancer researchers, those who bring fresh perspectives and innovative ideas to the field. By providing grants and funding to these researchers, The V Foundation is helping to ensure the continued advancement of cancer research. Additionally, the foundation supports research across all types of cancers, reflecting the complexity and diversity of the disease.

The impact of The V Foundation in the realm of cancer research is not just measured in terms of dollars raised and grants awarded. It is also seen in the progress made in cancer treatment, early detection, and patient care. The research funded by The V Foundation has contributed to significant advancements in understanding the biology of cancer, developing new therapies, and improving the quality of life for cancer patients. The foundation's work has been instrumental in pushing the boundaries of what is possible in cancer research, bringing hope to millions affected by the disease.

Jimmy Valvano's legacy in cancer research, embodied by The V Foundation, is a testament to his vision and his commitment to making a difference. The foundation's ongoing work continues to honor Valvano's memory and his message of hope, determination, and the relentless pursuit of dreams. Through its contributions to cancer research, The V Foundation stands as a beacon of hope in the fight against cancer, a cause that was deeply personal to Valvano and remains vital to countless individuals around the world.

## Enduring Message

The message that Jimmy Valvano imparted, centered on hope, perseverance, and living life to its fullest, continues to resonate and inspire long after his passing. His outlook on life, shaped by his personal experiences and his battle with cancer, has left an indelible mark on countless individuals. Valvano's philosophy, often encapsulated by his famous words, "Don't give up, don't ever give up," goes beyond the realm of sports and speaks to the universal human experience of facing and overcoming adversity.

Valvano's message of hope is one of his most powerful legacies. He believed in the importance of maintaining a positive outlook, even in the face of life's most challenging moments. This belief in hope was not about naïve optimism; rather, it was a recognition of the power of hope to provide strength and motivation during difficult times. Valvano's emphasis on hope has inspired individuals worldwide, encouraging them to hold onto their dreams and aspirations, regardless of the obstacles they may encounter.

Perseverance, another key aspect of Valvano's message, is a quality he embodied both in his coaching career and in his personal life. His determination to succeed and to keep moving forward despite setbacks is a lesson in resilience. Valvano's perseverance in the face of cancer, continuing to inspire and make a difference even as his health declined, is a demonstration of his strength of character. This aspect of his message encourages individuals to persist in their endeavors, to keep striving towards their goals, and to face challenges with courage and determination.

Living life to the fullest was a principle that Valvano passionately advocated. He believed in embracing life, experiencing it in all its dimensions, and finding joy in every moment. His advice to laugh, think, and have emotions move each day is a reminder of the richness of life and the importance of experiencing it deeply. Valvano's approach to life inspires individuals to appreciate the present, to engage fully with their experiences, and to cherish the relationships and opportunities they have.

Jimmy Valvano's enduring message continues to be a source of inspiration and guidance. It resonates not just with athletes and sports enthusiasts but with people from all walks of life who find strength and motivation in his words. Valvano's message is a call to embrace life with passion, to face challenges with hope and perseverance, and to make the most of every moment. His legacy lives on through his speeches, his foundation's work, and the countless lives he has touched, serving as a timeless beacon of inspiration and a reminder of the human spirit's resilience and capacity for joy.

# **LeBron James: From High School Phenom to NBA Superstar**

## Early Years and High School Fame

LeBron James' journey from a high school basketball prodigy to an NBA superstar is a tale of talent, hard work, and meteoric rise to fame. Born on December 30, 1984, in Akron, Ohio, LeBron's early life was filled with challenges, including financial instability and frequent moves. However, basketball became a stabilizing and central part of his life from a young age. His immense talent was evident early on and he quickly made a name for himself in the local basketball circuits.

LeBron attended St. Vincent-St. Mary High School in Akron, where he became a national sensation for his extraordinary basketball skills. His high school career was nothing short of phenomenal, marked by numerous accolades and widespread media attention. LeBron led his team to three state championships in four years, showcasing his ability to dominate games with his scoring, passing, and defensive prowess. His high school games began to attract large crowds and national media coverage, an unusual phenomenon for high school sports at the time.

LeBron's high school fame was not limited to his on-court performances. He was featured on the cover of "Sports Illustrated" magazine as a junior, with the title "The Chosen One," signaling his potential to be one of the greats in basketball. This level of attention and hype around a high school player was unprecedented, and LeBron was at the center of intense scrutiny and expectation. Despite this pressure, he continued to excel and improve, drawing comparisons to some of the greatest basketball players of all time.

LeBron's high school years were instrumental in shaping his future career. They were a period of growth, both as a player and as a person, under the intense glare of the national spotlight. His performances on the high school stage set the foundation for his future success and paved the way for his entry into the NBA. LeBron's early years and high school fame are evidence of his exceptional talent and his ability to handle the pressures of being in the public eye from a young age. His journey from a high school phenom to an NBA superstar began in the gyms of Akron, where he first displayed the talent and work ethic that would make him one of the most influential athletes in the world.

## NBA Draft and Rookie Season

LeBron James' entry into the NBA was as momentous as his high school career, marked by anticipation and excitement. In the 2003 NBA Draft, he was selected as the first overall pick by the Cleveland Cavaliers, a choice that was widely anticipated given his phenomenal talent and potential. LeBron's selection was significant not only for him personally but also for the Cavaliers, who were gaining a player already known as a once-in-a-generation talent. The 2003 draft itself was renowned for its depth of talent, with LeBron being part of a draft class that included other future NBA stars.

LeBron's transition to the NBA was highly scrutinized, with many wondering if he could live up to the lofty expectations set by his high school career. Any doubts, however, were quickly dispelled as he began his rookie season. LeBron made an immediate impact in the league, showcasing a level of skill and maturity that was extraordinary for a player straight out of high school. His debut game against the Sacramento Kings was a glimpse of what was to come; he scored 25 points, setting the record for the most points scored by a prep-to-pro player in his debut performance.

Throughout his rookie season, LeBron continued to impress both fans and critics. He demonstrated a well-rounded game, excelling in scoring, assists, and rebounds. His ability to impact the game in multiple ways and his basketball IQ were evident from the start. LeBron's performances were not just statistically impressive; they were also critical in improving the Cavaliers' competitiveness in the league. His presence brought a new energy to the team and reinvigorated the fan base.

The culmination of LeBron's remarkable rookie season was his winning of the NBA Rookie of the Year Award. This achievement was a testament to his hard work, talent, and the successful transition he had made from high school to professional basketball. LeBron finished his rookie season with averages of 20.9 points, 5.5 rebounds, and 5.9 assists per game, joining the likes of Michael Jordan and Oscar Robertson as the only players in NBA history to average at least 20 points, five rebounds, and five assists per game in their rookie season.

LeBron's draft into the NBA and his subsequent rookie season marked the beginning of what would become one of the most illustrious careers in basketball history. His ability to meet and exceed expectations, even under the immense pressure of being the first overall pick, set the stage for his future success in the league. LeBron's journey from a high school phenom to a successful NBA rookie showcased his extraordinary talent and his readiness to take on the challenges of professional basketball.

## Championships and MVP Awards

LeBron James' NBA career, marked by extraordinary achievements, reached new heights with his multiple NBA championships and MVP awards. These accolades not only underscored his individual brilliance but also his impact on team success. LeBron's journey to NBA championships began with a significant decision in 2010 to join the Miami Heat, forming a star-studded team alongside Dwyane Wade and Chris Bosh. This move was a turning point in his career and shifted the landscape of the NBA.

With the Miami Heat, LeBron's pursuit of an NBA championship was realized. He won his first NBA title in 2012, a momentous achievement that solidified his status as one of the game's greats. The Heat, under LeBron's leadership, defeated the Oklahoma City Thunder in the Finals. LeBron's performance throughout the season and the playoffs was exceptional, earning him the NBA Finals MVP award. He followed this up with another championship in 2013, where the Heat successfully defended their title against the San Antonio Spurs. LeBron once again was pivotal in the Finals, showcasing his versatility, basketball IQ, and clutch performances.

LeBron's return to the Cleveland Cavaliers in 2014 marked another significant chapter in his career. His decision to return to his home state was driven by a desire to bring a championship to

Cleveland. This dream was realized in 2016, in what is considered one of the greatest comebacks in NBA Finals history. The Cavaliers, led by LeBron, overcame a 3-1 deficit to defeat the Golden State Warriors. LeBron's performance in the series was historic and he was unanimously named Finals MVP, becoming the third player in NBA history to record a triple-double in a Finals Game 7.

In addition to his championships, LeBron has been recognized as the NBA's Most Valuable Player (MVP) four times (2009, 2010, 2012, 2013). These awards were evidence of his all-around excellence and his ability to elevate the performance of his teams. LeBron's MVP seasons were characterized by his dominance on both ends of the floor, his exceptional passing and scoring ability, and his leadership on and off the court.

LeBron's NBA championships and MVP awards are not just milestones in his career; they are reflections of his evolution as a player and his impact on the sport. His championships with both Miami and Cleveland showcased his ability to lead and excel in different team environments. Meanwhile, his MVP awards are indicative of his consistent excellence throughout his career and his status as one of the best players in the league. LeBron's achievements in winning multiple championships and MVP awards have solidified his legacy as one of the greatest basketball players of all time, a player who has left an indelible mark on the NBA.

## Off-Court Impact

LeBron James' influence extends far beyond the basketball court, with his off-court endeavors, particularly in philanthropy, highlighting his commitment to making a positive impact in the community. One of the most significant of these endeavors is the establishment of the I PROMISE School in his hometown of Akron, Ohio. This public school, a collaboration between the

LeBron James Family Foundation and Akron Public Schools, opened in 2018 and is designed to serve at-risk children by providing them with a stable and supportive learning environment.

The I PROMISE School is unique in its approach to education, focusing on the comprehensive needs of its students. It offers smaller class sizes, a longer school day, and a longer school year, aiming to provide more learning opportunities for the students. The curriculum is designed to be both rigorous and engaging, with a strong emphasis on science, technology, engineering, and mathematics (STEM) subjects, along with a focus on developing critical thinking and problem-solving skills.

Beyond the academic aspects, the I PROMISE School provides resources to address the social and emotional needs of its students. This includes a family resource center, which offers support for parents and families, including job placement assistance and legal aid. The school also provides free meals, uniforms, and transportation to students, alleviating some of the common barriers to education that students from disadvantaged backgrounds face.

LeBron's philanthropic work with the I PROMISE School is part of a broader commitment to giving back to his community. His foundation has been involved in various initiatives aimed at helping children and families in Akron. These initiatives include providing college scholarships, renovating community centers, and hosting annual events like bike-a-thons and Thanksgiving dinners for families in need.

LeBron's off-court impact through his philanthropic efforts speaks volumes about his character and his dedication to creating positive change. His investment in the I PROMISE School and other community initiatives reflects his understanding of the broader role he can play in society as a public figure and athlete. Through his actions, LeBron has shown a commitment to using his platform and resources to empower those in underprivileged communities, setting an example of how athletes can meaningfully contribute to social change. His work off the court, particularly with the I PROMISE School, is a testament to his belief in the power of education to transform lives and communities.

# The Story of Yao Ming

## Early Life in China

Yao Ming's journey to becoming an international basketball icon began in Shanghai, China, where he was born into a family with a strong basketball pedigree. His early life was intricately linked to the sport, with both of his parents being former professional basketball players in China. His father, Yao Zhiyuan, was a towering figure at 6 feet 7 inches (2 meters), and his mother, Fang Fengdi, stood an impressive 6 feet 3 inches (1.9 meters) tall, having been a captain of the Chinese national women's team. This basketball-centric family environment played a significant role in shaping Yao's future in the sport.

From an early age, Yao exhibited an unusual height and talent for basketball, attributes that were quickly recognized as potential for a future in professional sports. Given his parents' backgrounds and his own physical attributes, Yao was steered towards basketball from a young age. He started playing the game by the age of nine and it soon became evident that he was a prodigy. His height, combined with his natural talent, made him stand out among his peers.

Yao's formal training in basketball began when he was enrolled in the Shanghai Sports Institute, a prestigious institution known for nurturing athletic talent in China. At the Institute, Yao underwent rigorous training, which honed his skills and prepared him for a career in professional basketball. The training regime at the Institute was comprehensive, focusing not only on basketball skills but also on physical conditioning, tactical understanding, and mental fortitude.

Yao's time at the Shanghai Sports Institute was a crucial period in his development as a basketball player. It was here that he developed the fundamental skills that would later make him an international star. His height, which eventually reached 7 feet 6 inches (2.3 meters), combined with the skills he acquired during his training, made him a formidable player, attracting attention not just within China but from the international basketball community as well. Yao's early life in China, deeply rooted in basketball, laid the foundation for his rise to global fame, marking the beginning of a journey that would see him break barriers and become one of the most recognizable figures in the sport.

## Breaking into the NBA

Yao Ming's entry into the NBA marked a significant milestone in his career and the history of the league. In the 2002 NBA Draft, he was selected as the first overall pick by the Houston Rockets, a momentous occasion as he became the first international player ever to be drafted first without having previously played US college basketball. This selection was not only proof of Yao's immense talent and potential but also a sign of the NBA's growing global reach.

Yao's transition to the NBA was met with immense curiosity and high expectations. Being the first overall pick came with its own set of pressures, and Yao was stepping into a league that was vastly different from what he had experienced in China. The NBA's style of play was more physical and fast-paced, presenting a new set of challenges for Yao to adapt to. Additionally, there were cultural and language barriers that Yao had to navigate as he moved from China to the United States, adding to the complexities of his transition.

In his rookie season with the Rockets, Yao faced the challenge of proving himself in a league filled with the world's best players. There was skepticism from some quarters about his ability to compete at the highest level, given the perceived differences in the quality of basketball between the NBA and the Chinese Basketball Association (CBA). However, Yao quickly began to dispel these doubts with his performances on the court. He showed that he could hold his own against the NBA's top talents, bringing a unique combination of size, skill, and basketball IQ to the game.

Yao's impact as a rookie was significant. He brought a new dimension to the Rockets' gameplay, offering a strong presence in the paint both offensively and defensively. His ability to score, rebound, and block shots made him a key player for the team. Off the court, Yao's arrival in the NBA was a cultural phenomenon. He attracted a huge following, not just in the United States but also back home in China, where millions of fans stayed up late to watch his games. His presence in the league contributed to a surge in the NBA's popularity in China, opening up a massive new market for the league.

Yao Ming's breaking into the NBA as the first overall pick was a groundbreaking moment that transcended sports. It highlighted the global nature of basketball and paved the way for more international players to make their mark in the league. Yao's successful adaptation to the NBA, despite the initial challenges, set a precedent and served as an inspiration for future generations of international players aspiring to play at the highest level of basketball.

## Success and Cultural Impact

Yao Ming's success in the NBA extended beyond his impressive statistics and accolades on the court. His career had a profound cultural impact, particularly in bridging the gap between the NBA and China, and significantly boosting the league's global appeal. As Yao established himself as a dominant force in the league, he simultaneously became a cultural ambassador, fostering a deeper connection between the NBA and his home country, China.

On the court, Yao's achievements were noteworthy. He was an eight-time NBA All-Star, a testament to his skill, popularity, and the respect he garnered from fans and peers alike. His ability to compete with the best in the league elevated his status as one of the top centers in the NBA. Yao's playing style, which combined traditional center play with a soft shooting touch, challenged the stereotypes often associated with big men in basketball. His presence in the paint was formidable and he was known for his sportsmanship, professionalism, and the respect he commanded from teammates and opponents alike.

Off the court, Yao's influence was even more significant. He became a symbol of the growing relationship between the NBA and China, a relationship that has since become a crucial part of the NBA's international strategy. Yao's games were broadcast to millions of fans in China, bringing NBA basketball into the homes of a vast audience. His popularity helped to popularize the sport in China, leading to an increased interest in basketball among the Chinese youth, the development of basketball programs, and a surge in NBA merchandise sales in the country.

Yao's role in increasing the NBA's global appeal was marked by his ability to resonate with fans not just as an athlete but as a cultural icon. He carried the expectations and hopes of millions of Chinese fans, serving as a bridge between two distinct basketball cultures. His humble demeanor, combined with his success, made him a beloved figure in both the United States and China. Yao's unique position as a cultural link between the East and the West was instrumental in expanding the NBA's reach and contributing to its status as a global sports league.

Yao Ming's impact on the NBA and basketball's global appeal can be seen in the increasing number of international players in the league and the growing interest in basketball around the world. He opened doors for other international players and showed that talent from any part of the world could shine in the NBA. Yao's legacy extends beyond his playing career; his influence on the cultural and global aspects of basketball continues to be felt, underlining his importance not just as a player but as an ambassador of the sport.

## Retirement and Legacy

Yao Ming's retirement from professional basketball in 2011, prompted by a series of injuries, marked the end of a remarkable playing career but not the conclusion of his influence in the world of basketball. His decision to retire at the age of 30 came after a series of foot and ankle injuries that hindered his ability to play at the highest level. Yao's departure from the NBA was a significant moment, not just for his fans and the Houston

Rockets, but for the global basketball community. His impact on the sport, however, continued to grow even after his retirement, as he transitioned into roles that allowed him to influence the game from beyond the court.

Yao's legacy in basketball is multifaceted. As a player, he left an indelible mark on the NBA and international basketball. His success as one of the first Chinese players in the NBA opened the door for other international players and helped to globalize the sport. Yao's career challenged perceptions about international players and demonstrated the global talent pool available to the NBA. His unique blend of size, skill, and intelligence on the court redefined what was expected of a center, influencing the next generation of big men in the game.

Beyond his playing career, Yao has played a significant role in basketball administration and as a global ambassador for the sport. He has been actively involved in promoting basketball in China and around the world. In 2016, Yao was elected as the president of the Chinese Basketball Association (CBA), a role that has allowed him to influence the development of basketball in his home country significantly. Under his leadership, the CBA has implemented reforms to improve the quality of the league and to promote the development of young Chinese players.

Yao's involvement in basketball goes beyond administrative roles. He has been a global ambassador for the sport, participating in various initiatives to promote basketball across the world. His presence and influence have been instrumental in fostering international relationships and in promoting cultural exchange through basketball. Yao's philanthropic efforts have also been notable, particularly in education and wildlife conservation.

Yao Ming's legacy in basketball is enduring. His impact is not just measured in his on-court achievements but also in his contributions to the growth and development of the sport globally. His journey from a young player in Shanghai to an NBA star and basketball administrator is a testament to his passion for the game and his commitment to using his platform to make a positive impact. Yao's legacy continues to inspire and influence, both in China and globally, as he remains a respected and influential figure in the world of basketball.

## The Legend of Michael Jordan

### Early Challenges and College Success

Michael Jordan's path to becoming a basketball legend was not without its initial setbacks and challenges, which played a crucial role in shaping his storied career. One of the most well-known anecdotes from Jordan's early life is his failure to make the varsity basketball team during his sophomore year at Emsley A. Laney High School in Wilmington, North Carolina. This rejection, often cited as a pivotal moment in Jordan's life, fueled his determination to succeed and become a better player. He used this setback as motivation, dedicating himself to rigorous practice and improvement. The following year, he made the varsity team and quickly established himself as a standout player, showcasing his talent and work ethic.

Jordan's high school success led to a scholarship at the University of North Carolina (UNC) at Chapel Hill, where he played under legendary coach Dean Smith. At UNC, Jordan's skills continued to flourish. He was named ACC Freshman of the Year in 1982, showcasing his immediate impact on the team. His time at UNC was marked by significant growth, both as a player and as a team contributor. Jordan was known for his scoring ability, defensive prowess, and his capacity to play under pressure – traits that would become hallmarks of his professional career.

The crowning moment of Jordan's college career came in the 1982 NCAA Championship game against Georgetown University. In a closely contested game, with UNC trailing by one point, Jordan made the iconic game-winning jump shot with just 17 seconds left on the clock. This shot is not only remembered as the highlight of the 1982 NCAA Tournament but also as a defining moment in Jordan's career, symbolizing his clutch performance under pressure and his emergence as a top player. It was a precursor to the numerous game-winning shots and clutch performances that would define his career in the NBA.

Jordan's early challenges, followed by his college success and the iconic shot to win the 1982 NCAA Championship, laid the foundation for his ascent to basketball immortality. These experiences at Laney High School and UNC shaped his competitive spirit, his relentless pursuit of excellence, and his ability to rise to the occasion when it mattered most. This early period of Jordan's life and career is a reflection of his resilience and determination, qualities that would propel him to become one of the greatest athletes in the history of sports.

## NBA Domination and First Retirement

Michael Jordan's entry into the NBA began with the Chicago Bulls drafting him third overall in the 1984 NBA Draft, a decision that would dramatically alter the franchise's destiny and the landscape of the league. Jordan's impact was immediate and profound; he finished his rookie season with an average of 28.2 points per game and earned the NBA Rookie of the Year Award. His remarkable athleticism, scoring ability, and competitive drive quickly turned him into one of the most exciting players to watch in the league.

As Jordan's career progressed with the Bulls, he evolved from a high-scoring guard into the face of the NBA. His ability to dominate games, coupled with his flair for dramatic, high-flying plays, made him a favorite among fans and a nightmare for opponents. Jordan led the league in scoring for seven consecutive seasons from 1986 to 1993, highlighting his offensive prowess and ability to consistently perform at an elite level.

The pinnacle of Jordan's career with the Bulls came in the form of the team's first three-peat of NBA championships from 1991 to 1993. These championship victories were not just a testament to Jordan's individual brilliance but also his ability to elevate the play of his teammates. The first championship in 1991 was particularly significant as it established the Bulls as a powerhouse in the NBA and provided Jordan with his long-sought validation as a winner. The 1992 and 1993 championships further cemented the Bulls' dominance in the league and Jordan's status as the game's premier player.

In a move that shocked the sports world, Michael Jordan announced his first retirement from basketball in October 1993. This decision came at the height of his career, following his father's tragic death and amidst growing pressures and scrutiny in his professional life. Jordan's retirement sent ripples through the NBA, as he had become synonymous with the sport. His departure from basketball was a significant moment, marking the end of a dominant era for the Bulls and leaving fans and players alike wondering what the future held for both Jordan and the league.

Jordan's first retirement from the NBA marked the end of a chapter characterized by individual accolades, team success, and a transformative impact on the sport. His rise to superstardom with the Bulls and the subsequent three-peat of championships had elevated him to an iconic status, while his sudden retirement added an unexpected twist to an already legendary career. This period of Jordan's life encapsulates his journey from a promising young talent to a global sports icon and the abrupt pause that left the basketball world in anticipation of his next move.

## Baseball Career and NBA Comeback

Michael Jordan's foray into professional baseball following his first retirement from the NBA was an unexpected turn in his sporting journey. In February 1994, Jordan signed a minor league baseball contract with the Chicago White Sox, an affiliate of the Birmingham Barons. His decision to switch sports was influenced by a childhood dream and his father's love for baseball. While Jordan's baseball career was met with mixed reactions and varying degrees of success, it showcased his willingness to challenge himself and step out of his comfort zone.

During his time with the Barons, Jordan displayed commendable effort and a strong work ethic, but it became clear that his prowess on the baseball field did not match his basketball dominance. He played as an outfielder and had a batting average of .202, with 3 home runs, 51 RBIs, and 30 stolen bases. Despite not reaching the same heights in baseball as he did in basketball, Jordan's stint in the sport demonstrated his competitive spirit and his dedication to pursuing his personal goals.

Jordan's return to the NBA in March 1995 marked the beginning of another extraordinary chapter in his basketball career. Announcing his comeback with a famous two-word press release, "I'm back," Jordan rejoined the Chicago Bulls towards the end of the 1994-1995 season. His return reignited excitement in the

NBA and fans eagerly anticipated his return to the court. While the Bulls were eliminated in the playoffs that season, it set the stage for what would be another remarkable run of success.

The 1995-1996 season marked the start of the Bulls' second three-peat of championships, with Jordan at the forefront. He led the Bulls to an NBA record 72 wins during the regular season and was named the league's Most Valuable Player. The Bulls dominated the playoffs and won the NBA championship, a triumphant return for Jordan. The subsequent two seasons, 1996-1997 and 1997-1998, saw the Bulls continue their dominance, winning two more championships and solidifying their legacy as one of the greatest teams in NBA history.

Jordan's comeback to the NBA and the Bulls' second three-peat symbolized his resilience, determination, and enduring skill. His brief baseball career and subsequent return to basketball highlight a period in his life characterized by personal challenges, a pursuit of dreams, and a triumphant return to the pinnacle of his sport. This phase of Jordan's career further cemented his status as not just a basketball legend, but a global sports icon known for his remarkable ability to succeed, adapt, and excel in the face of new challenges.

## Legacy and Cultural Impact

Michael Jordan's legacy as one of the greatest basketball players of all time is undisputed and his influence extends far beyond the basketball court into popular culture and the business world. Jordan's impact on the game of basketball is monumental; he revolutionized the sport with his extraordinary talent, competitive spirit, and his ability to perform under pressure. His six NBA championships and five MVP awards speak to his dominance, but his influence is also measured in how he changed the perception of basketball players as global icons.

Jordan's cultural impact is as significant as his athletic achievements. He became a cultural icon, transcending sports and becoming a household name around the world. His partnership with Nike and the creation of the Air Jordan brand revolutionized sports marketing and the sneaker industry. The Air Jordan brand became a symbol of style, performance, and excellence, and it continues to be a dominant force in the market. Jordan's influence in fashion, particularly in the realm of athletic wear, is profound and enduring.

In popular culture, Michael Jordan became a figure of inspiration and admiration. He was the subject of numerous endorsements and television appearances, and even led the cast of the movie "Space Jam," which blended the worlds of basketball and entertainment. His competitive nature and dedication to excellence made him a role model for athletes and non-athletes alike. Jordan's story of overcoming challenges, striving for greatness, and achieving his dreams resonates with people of different ages and backgrounds.

Beyond his playing days, Jordan's influence in the sport and business of basketball continues. He became the first former NBA player to become the majority owner of a league franchise, the Charlotte Hornets. His involvement in team ownership and management demonstrates his ongoing commitment to the sport and his desire to impact the game from a different perspective. Jordan's voice and opinion in the realm of basketball and sports, in general, carry significant weight, highlighting his enduring presence in the industry.

Michael Jordan's legacy is multifaceted. As a player, he was a relentless competitor and a winner. As a cultural icon, he is a symbol of excellence and global recognition. In the business world, he is an innovator and a trailblazer. His impact on basketball, popular culture, and the business of sports is profound and lasting. Jordan's journey from a high school player who was cut from his team to becoming a global icon is a story of determination, talent, and the relentless pursuit of greatness. His legacy continues to inspire and influence, making him a permanent fixture in the annals of sports history and beyond.

# References

Goodwin, Dale. Title IX: Five Decades of Positive Changes on Gonzaga Women's Sports Scene. Gonzaga University (2023). https://www.gonzaga.edu/news-events/stories/2023/2/2/title-ix-journey-for-women-in-sports. Accessed December 02, 2023

Harris, Richard. 'Stephen Curry: Underrated' documentary tells his Davidson College origin story. Andscape (2023). https://andscape.com/features/stephen-curry-underrated-documentary-tells-his-davidson-college-origin-story/. Accessed November 29, 2023.

Knapp, Fritz. Jim Valvano: Joyfulness. Price World Publishing (2012).

Milazzo, Brit. Jason "J-Mac" McElwain: Autism, Basketball and Life Without Limits. Bleacher Report (2009). https://bleacherreport.com/articles/121162-life-without-limits. Accessed December 03, 2023.

Motin, Adam. The Legend of Michael Jordan, Triumph Books (2020)

Sielski, Mike. The Rise: Kobe Bryant and the Pursuit of Immortality. Pan Macmillan (2022).

Tanniyom, Maruak. Yao Ming: The NBA star made by the order of the Chinese Government | Main Stand. Bleacher Report (2022). https://mainstand.co.th/en/features/5/article/3252#google_vignette. Accessed December 03, 2023

The New York Times Editorial Staff. LeBron James. The New York Times Editorial Staff (2019).

## Bonus: Free Book!

Are you ready to delve into the thrilling book in the series, absolutely free? Get ready to go deep into the world of yet another football legend! Just use your smartphone or tablet to scan the QR code below, then follow the simple prompts to receive the PDF.

www.ingramcontent.com/pod-product-compliance
Lightning Source LLC
Chambersburg PA
CBHW052104110526
44591CB00013B/2342